Hardscrabble

Life on the Land

Hardscrabble

Life on the Land

Wes Hanson

月亮

CAVE MOON PRESS

YAKIMA 中 WASHINGTON

cavemoonpress.com 中 cavemoonpress@gmail.com

Preface

The Carder family has owned Carder Farm for 125 years. Its 160 acres contain old growth firs and pines. The last heavy logging was done ninety years ago using cross-cut saws and horses. A 30-acre meadow with wetlands provides habitats for numerous songbirds, waterfowl, hawks and owls. Coyotes, deer, elk, moose, cougars and bears use it and the woods. This rich habitat lies two miles from busy downtown Coeur d'Alene. The farm is permanently protected by a conservation easement.

I married into the family 50 years ago and through labor and observation have come to intimately know and love this land. I have felled many trees for firewood and lumber and harvested hay. Nature's complexity--from fidgeting wrens, to marauding moose, to soaring red-tailed hawks—enriches me. To capture these things, I write poems, draw and paint watercolors.

My in-laws, Alvis and Marguerite Carder, called the farm Hardscrabble Hill. Alvis spent his life working as a logger and in lumber mills. They built the farmhouse in 1935. Alvis and Marguerite raised three children, including my deceased wife, Gertie. The family relied on a large garden, some cattle and a milk cow for food. Shortly before I married Gertie, Alvis died in a logging accident. After that, Marguerite and I chased cattle who found a hole in fencing, as they often do. This was my baptism.

All the Carders were committed to the farm's preservation. In 1997, Gertie signed a conservation easement to prevent further development. I am now the farm's caretaker.

The poems are arranged in a seasonal order. Spring announces life's awakening. Summer celebrates growth. Fall chronicles decline, and Winter focuses on rest and preparation for renewal. Most of the poems are dated by year. The undated poems are lost in time.

I hope these poems convey the discoveries, struggles and joys I have experienced.

Dedication

I dedicate this book to Alvis and Marguerite Carder, to my deceased wife Gertie, and to my partner Theresa Shaffer.

Contents

Beginning

3   How the Farm Is

4   The Land

5   Soul Matters

Spring

9   March

9   April

9   May

9   Warm Tea

10   Two

11   Counting

12   Fire

13   Spring

14   On Sunday

15   Working on the Ford 2N Tractor

16   Antidote for Contagion

17   Monday Morning

18   Separate

19   Accoutrements

20   The Unexpected

20   The Unexpected 2

21   Against

22   Sauntering

23   This Afternoon

24   The Is

Summer

27   June
27   July
27   August
28   Quail and Others
29   Men in Time
31   At War
32   Harvest
33   One Circle
34   Small Acts
35   I Tell You
36   Piecemeal
36   Coming Close
37   Gift
38   Desultory
39   In the Aviary
40   Revealed
41   Moose
42   August 14 Between the House and Barn
43   Nighthawk
44   Old Cars
45   Back Seat, Musty Plymouth
46   Responses to Drought
47   Breakfast Early

Fall

51   September
51   October
51   November
52   Overlook
53   Boundaries
54   Yard Inventory

55 This Evening

56 Crossbedding

57 How Quickly

58 Tallies

59 Old World Opening

60 Tree

61 Meanderings

62 Variation on the Theme of Soup

63 Orchard Girl

64 Midafternoon, Evening November

65 Love and a 2N Tractor

66 To the Woods

67 Ice Storm

68 On Watching Geese

Winter

71 December

71 January

71 February

72 First Snow

73 Languor

74 Winter Morning

75 Meadow, 6:43 A.M.

76 Projections

77 Two Astronomers Ski the Meadow

78 Full Circle

79 On This Morning

80 All This

81 My Mother-in-Law

Onward

85   Last Morning

86   Light Left the Meadow

87   Days End

88   On This Day

89   Acknowledgment

90   About the Author

Beginning

How the Farm Is

Let me tell you how the farm is.
The dog shows up,
Shaking off water from the weeds.
She leans against the sliding door.

I finish breakfast.

Swallows glide in and out of sunlight.
My wife's coffee, boiling in an enamel pan,
Flows over the lip and hisses through the burner.

I call the dog's name, call again.
Her eyes stare at me through the glass.
I cinch bootlaces and slide suspenders on,
Grab my felt hat.

By now she is frenzied.
Racing down the steps
She scatters juncos.
Morning has begun.

The Land

The more I simply am—
Listening to robins before dawn,
Watching toms court hens,
Feeling bark where nuthatches search—
I sense how much my life is one
With place, this place,
Its vernal ponds
Where peepers chant in unison
And swallows soar blue sky.

I used to think I could control its course
Through logging trees and tilling fields
But found myself carried by renewal.

What have I learned?
A man has more with less.
Nature yields kaleidoscopic wealth.

2022

Soul Matters

Let us begin with words,
Words that suggest, connect
Not with things important
But with common moments—
I mean a Steller's jay
Cocking its head as it probes a feeder,
Its iridescent flight to a bare limb and raucous calls,
I mean a swallow tipping on a wire,
A house wren singing to the audience of sun.
I mean the haste of turning from a love
We might embrace.
The nonchalance we make of fledging things
That held might deepen us.

Spring

March

Month of transitions—
Winter birds feeding with arrivals.
Light brightening windows.

April

As snow crust melts,
I prune broken branches,
Opening tree hearts.

May

Wind stirs leaves,
Birds grip limbs,
Bobbing before flying.

Warm Tea

Thick frost outside reminds me of late snow,
Yet this is March.
I hold a teacup in cold hands.

2013

Two

Before dawn two great horned owls call,
One far away, the other near,
In spring fog, hoots turn to dialog.
One, questioned, replies. This goes on.
I listen closely for nuance, because I am human
And must guess to know. Growing light awakens
Flicker calls and small bird songs,
But in deep woods slow muffled hoots.

2016

Counting

Dawn.
Gobbles, spreading feathers
And what's invisible belong,
Are counted in day's tally.

Cool breeze fluffs curtains
And you ask about the sounds.

I say, Just toms and hens about their business,
Turf wars and wild cavorting,
Feathered flagships breasting
A cold spring morning.

2023

Fire

I placed crumpled paper on ash embers,
Stacked kindling, lit paper, shut the stove door
And walked through the house.
Halfway up the stairs, smoke burst to flame.

At that, I questioned fixed routines.
Why these each morning? My legs have spring.
Warped fingers can be acrobats. I imagined
Dancing on the narrow steps.

Fear is losing the will to climb, falling to the body's pull,
Surrendering the mind to fate—
All nixed when new thought quickens.

Flames grew.
This is how dark brightens.
This is how a cold house warms.
This is how the old find vital heat.

2018

Spring

Frost heaves ground.
Dead weeds bend with crystals.
Deer weave through trees,
Almost invisible
Until sun lights tan fur.

I should spread seeds in the meadow
And till them in. I should transplant the plum tree
To the orchard. Birdhouses are cleaned.
Garden beds need turning.

Underground, root movement,
Seeds sprouting, soil split
By pale stems.

2013

On Sunday

I walk on the logging road beneath the power line--
Past the stake truck with flat tires, a '36 Ford flathead
With cracked windows, bullet-riddled doors
And rusty seat springs—to the mailbox.

In the box some letters addressed to the current resident,
That's me. One offers to buy my house for cash, as if
I need cash to go on living. A postcard from a friend
Says her husband died. He was my friend.
I laughed with him, enjoyed his laugh.

Behind me a car roars by.
Being Sunday, people flock,
Listen to bells rung, words spun,
Their sins forgiven.

Here, the new sun beckons
And stirs things more promiscuous.
What is that bird that hops and disappears,
That bush's name where the bird has hopped?
How does light wind feel?
How long will ice stay frozen?

Walking home, I step on ice which slides.
Does it resemble time unlocked?
I would rather be ambushed by surprise,
By what is heard-felt-seen
Than what is known.

2022

Working on the Ford 2N Tractor

We hover over the running engine
Listening to tappets click,
Inhaling oil drips on the manifold.
You finger linkage. The engine revs.
I watch your face. You know much more than me.
You shout over the clatter and point at something.
I nod, not sure what you said,
But glad to stand beside you
As we breathe hot fumes.

2015

Antidote to Contagion

Wash hands often.
Wear a mask.
Shun crowds.
Stay home.

I went to pick up mail,
Being careful holding envelopes.

Walking home I looked at treetops,
Red firs and ponderosa pines,
And spotted, after years of roaming,
A white pine.

I walked to it crowded by two firs
And wondered how it grew there
Far from other pines. White pitch
Flowed down its trunk and low branches
Offered rungs for thoughts. I climbed high
Into needles and wind, feeling the trunk lever,
Bend, return, far off from the contagion in our midst.

2020

Monday Morning

One wakes on Monday morning
Before dawn to wrens' fluting songs
And chickadees repeating what they're called.

For a while a dove's hushed coos
Flow from tree shadows.

Before the rising sun claims day
Like truth announced at noon.

2006

Separate

Gordon Tate swung his lantern to survey the cows
And say goodnight.
He shut the door and turned the wooden latch,
No need for locks in the country.
He crossed the yard with his mutt trotting at his heels
And stopped to look in at nesting hens.
He paused to notice moonlight turn the farmyard
Into shadowed shapes. The barn, for instance,
Became large shouldered over man and dog.
Indoors, he gave the dog a treat
And pet as it rubbed his jeans.
How easily dogs sleep, he thought,
And snuffed the lantern flame
As moonlight filled the kitchen.

2013

Accoutrements

Earmuffed, goggled, gloved,
I weed whack between fruit trees.
Apples emerge from buds
After bees daub blossoms.

The impulse to slash grass controls
Until I see a swallowtail flutter
Among leaves and question labor's purpose.

Grass grows. A butterfly without appointment
Dips and rises, breeze-borne and by impulse.
I, feeling compelled by busyness and urge,
Swing the trimmer head to vanquish what?

This question does not need an answer.
The butterfly lands on a wild rose and sups.

2021

The Unexpected

A swallowtail flutters
Across gray siding
And suddenly monotony is razed
By dithering.

2013

The Unexpected 2

A friend who knows the farm
Even more than I do
Said he stood in the meadow
As a fawn and young coyote
Emerged from the woods.
They ran in circles, teased and charged—
Unaware of what they were.

2013

Against

I woke to robins singing before dawn
And wind whispering through the screen.
Something holy coexists as close as feathers
Touching air.

A poem states what sense suggests.
How smug.
The robin hops, jabs grass.
It states what's real with insistent stabs.

I sense what is but cannot hold what lives.
Singing stops.
Wind undulates the eastern curtain.
Light plies with shadow.
I search for words to pin what passes
With a certain statement—
As if thought could arrest,
As if robins could be statues,
As if wind could gel
As if the sun might be ornamental.

2021

Sauntering

This morning, we walk logging roads
That follow slopes and curves, opening and closing
Where trees grow. Thistles have fluffed.
Knapweed stalks cross tire ruts.
Time to blend, to leave our cares.

You point at blackberry vines.
For a while we find rhythm.
The slough beside us is pock-marked
Where deer crossed. I snap hanging branches
And push a rotted log aside.
A ruffed grouse explodes and glides
Through snarled brush.

You stop, startled.

I find a path through dog-hair trees
And step over bear scat, talking.
No need to surprise it.

We meander.
I pull some knapweed to retard its spread.
Red firs are thinning, dying.
Next year's firewood,
But this morning we concentrate on now,
The near, what stirs and what is sensed.

This Afternoon

This afternoon I wade through thigh-high grass,
Surprised my cuffs aren't damp with dew.
The meadow lies untilled,
Going back to trees.
I should cut saplings to keep the field
Past labor cleared.

The wild encroaches.
Elk pellets dot the grass tracks the pickup made.
Juncos flit and land in weeds.

My fingertips brush grass tips.
I think of plows and disks,
The promise of seeds spread and pressed,
Green, uniform across the field,
Grass cut, turned, baled,
Shaved stubble.

I think about what's wild,
Bounding deer, the red-tail's screech
And imagine the unseen that makes the meadow.

The Is

Gray feathers cross green grass.
A bird flies nearby.
If I think robin, I ignore its red breast,
Or call it valiant, vain,
Compare it to Napoleon,
Then I miss what should compel:
Hops, head tilts, stabs,
A worm stretched,
Snapped up, choked down,
And quick, short bounds—
The very things that constitute what's real.

2013

Summer

June

We plant seeds,
Cover them and tamp,
Side by side like monks.

July

Nothing moves at dawn
Until a deer walks through,
Browsing, staring.

August

Leaves curling,
My throat parched,
Pending wildfire.

Quail and Others

Still morning.
Boot strides through drooped weeds
Stir a dozen quail. They beat wings
In unison, glide to safety and resume
Feeding under dappled leaves.

Ahead, a pocket gopher's dirt mound
Where a grouse dusted.
I stride on until a flushed grouse bursts
Through thick twigs and glides down.

And so it is. Disturbance prompts results.
In the meadow deer browse in canary grass.
They spot me, and in bounds
Flagging white scuts vanish.

2022

Men in Time

Rex and I spend a sweaty afternoon
Clearing brush and following road ruts
Below Nighthawk Hill.
He talks about the time he and Alvis
Hauled logs off the farm
Using cross-cut saws and horses.

We pull snarled limbs and chop out ocean spray
That pours in white waves over us.

"You know the Sliding Gate's near here," Rex says.
"The Sliding Gate," I ask.
"What's that?"

"Ya," Rex grunts. He grunts loud when he talks.
"They had the gate to keep cows out."

I look at tangled growth.

Rex bends, hitching his lame leg
In wobbling steps. He chops and rocks for balance
As he goes. I stand balanced.

Rex yanks a log that breaks in red decay
And falls back into brush.

"Damn legs," he says. "No good."

I keep on working.
I find in silence what the forest says.

Today at least Rex comes back cutting low.
I cut larger logs and pull them out.

This afternoon we labor deep in woods.

At War

This year pocket gophers tunnel near fruit trees.
Each morning, I survey fresh mounds.
They have their role excavating, aerating ground.
The problems are odds and tolerance.

I have set traps and baited them with oats.
The score is ten escapes to one.
The traps are often sprung or dug around.

Still, I scan for fresh dirt mounds,
Probe for tunnels, dig and place traps
Both directions.

The odds are always long, like searching
For owls in dark woods.

I admire pocket gophers
That burrow rocky ground
And gnaw dirt-clogged roots.

But tolerance has died,
And I, armed with wire probes,
A trowel and tangled traps,
Kneel to excavate.
I place traps near a plum tree,
Cover them with a board and wait.
Trench warfare in the orchard springs its trap.

2017

Harvest

Before I get to the meadow
I hear the baler's rhythmic sounds.
It silences bird calls at twilight.
My neighbor drives his tractor,
Glancing back as bales drop.
With enough, he stops and joins me.

As we walk beside the flat-bed trailer
That his wife tows,
We toss bales, stack
And cinch them.
Then his wife drives to the barn,
Slowly rocking through the field.

2022

One Circle

Last year the meadow lay fallow.
Grass waved in wind and carried uneven snow.
In spring I walked beaten grass
And saw green shoots emerge.

In July my neighbor mowed the field,
Windrowed hay, baled it and hauled.

In the fall I cut out sprouting pines
And tilled to plant new seeds.

The sun rides through the sky.
The meadow is an oval.

I ride the tractor's springy seat
And turn the steering wheel.
In this small world the circle is complete.

2007

Small Acts

Last night I watered bolting lettuce.
A bald-faced hornet buzzed my face.
I brushed it away. It landed on carrot leaves.
I sprayed to kill it, to punish it for who knows what,
Continued as it tried to fly and watched it curl up,
Moving slowly. I had mixed feelings.
What had I done? Killed a tiny creature because I could?
Then I remembered being stung by a bald-faced hornet
On the brow and watching it swell until it closed my eye.
Perhaps this is why I punished this curled hornet.

I stopped spraying and parted carrot tops to watch
Its legs twitch. I pushed the hornet to drier dirt,
Being careful because memory still stung, and coaxed it
Till its wings spread.
Satisfied, I left it, hoping it would fly.

This morning as I moved the sprinkler,
I checked the garden where vengeance stopped
And felt dirt beside carrots.

2007

I Tell You

A day ago, two dappled fawns
Ran through the headlights without a doe.
You thought they were abandoned.

I worried about marauding dogs,
But I thought, too, the fawns were old enough to feed.

Then we both forgot. You know how life veers
Quickly like two fawns through woods.

This morning, we spotted two fawns
With a doe. They browsed easily on summer grass.
The world goes on.

2015

Piecemeal

Woodchips in my hair,
A smudge of resin on my thumb,
Aching arches,
The sound of fiber ripping from a stump,
The ooze of pine pitch flowing from a cut,
The way the woods resume when I am done.

Coming Close

The whirring chain teeth chewed through bark
And sprayed wood chips and sawdust on my chaps.
I rocked the saw and slabbed off rounds.
They rolled. I kicked them from my path.
Ambition for firewood obsessed.
I moved along the trunk,
Trimming limbs, cutting butts,
Thinking of cold days ahead until I stopped the chainsaw
And nature's sounds returned—a flicker drilling somewhere,
A nuthatch's pugnacious jeers, a feisty wren
Reclaiming its domain when I went home.

2018

Gift

The dandelion seed drifts on wind,
The physical and invisible attuned.
I tried to catch it, but it flew from swipes.
What is beyond us cannot be caught,
Lingers, tempts, like beauty out of reach
Or love's lure that escapes.
I watched the seed land,
Perhaps to grow next spring,
Perhaps to turn to dust on stony ground.

2018

Desultory

Yesterday, before the sun baked the day,
I climbed the ladder headed to the roof
Planning to clean chimneys.
Halfway up, on the back deck
I saw a chickadee, a carcass really, splayed.
I pieced evidence and guessed it flew
Into the window reflecting sky,
Broke its neck and died.
I climbed the ladder with different thought,
No longer so intent on cleaning.

2018

In the Aviary

Robin calls opened dawn on the plowed field.
Where later juncos pecked at clods.
Chickadees crowded feeders
While the wren sang melodies
And shuttled between twig-stuffed houses.

At noon stout ravens landed on the roof,
Spooking a flicker. But being brutes,
Without anyone to bully, the ravens left.
Meanwhile, the wren flew to nearby brush
Where it scolded swooping swallows.

In late afternoon magpies hopped
Among smaller birds like robbers
And in thick woods
A mourning dove cooed pensively,
Alone.

2013

Revealed

Odd how when you look you see
Things overlooked.
As this morning drying off after showering,
I saw a violet-green swallow balancing
On chicken wire strung around the garden.

As the other day turning on a spigot,
I focused on a spider web strung
Where siding angled.
There, wrapped mosquitos
And dandelion seeds hung.
I bent and blew the web.
The spider dashed to snare what hit.
I stepped back to watch life weave a story.

And as this morning, awake,
I listened to you breathe
And watched your thoughts express.
You pursed your lips, relaxed.

2017

Moose

Raining hard with streams pouring from the roof
And apple leaves tapped by drops,
The bush by the wren house moves,
Leaves thrashing.

A nibbling deer spooks
And runs past the orchard.

Dark legs poke down through branches,
Dark legs beneath tossed limbs.

A moose calf emerges.
More legs follow—its mother
And under her a twin.

One calf jabs teats.
The other strips leaves.
The mother stands
Tugging higher branches.

2013

August 14 Between the House and Barn

Ravens caw to panic fledgling birds.
Nothing new about a gang—
Black suits, dark minds,
Weak hoods in search of prey
To puff bravado.

At first, I thought they gathered to cavort
But watched them wield and flare around a point.
The wind was up. I must have missed
The cries of death, raw tearing
Before parting.

2021

Nighthawk

We climbed on crumbling stones above the barn
And left the ordered farm. Downed wire
Marked the midway point. Above, dead snags
And evening sky.

It was growing dark,
The time when birds give way to bats.
We stood small on the swollen hill
And looked toward the horizon.
I felt like an explorer, and you?

Overhead, a nighthawk fluttered and dove
To chase us from its nest, we thought.

We descended, picking around rocks,
Remembering where wires crossed,
To the barn, to the familiar,
Where we walked.

2022

Old Cars

Two Plymouths stuck in alders growing through bumpers
Have cracked glass and ripped cloth seats and springs.
I lean on a door and imagine what occurred—
Leg tangled love, roaring around a curve, voices and dialed static.
These are inventions. Who can animate what's gone?

One Plymouth is from the 1930's, the other after that.
Their engines flathead sixes. One glove box holds curled papers.
Their owners are dead. I wonder how they got here,
Imprisoned by dense trees.
Who can assemble acts when they are done?
I crumble moss on glass and chrome.

2016

Back Seat, Musty Plymouth

Not because I love cobwebs or mold,
I open the rusty door and sit in the car's back seat.
Old cars turn into relics and are crushed.
But in a pine thicket the Plymouth on blocks
Holds what might possibly have been—
Moonlight filtering through leaves,
Glass steamed and rubbed in September,
Soft talk and urgency,
Or children poking fingers into ribs
And later sleeping on velour
With a window cracked
And the wind whispering
To children imagining what could be.

I watch a spider drop on self-made line
And wander on the cushion where it landed,
As if inventing is the way it lives.

Inventing? The motor roars.
I steer through trees.

2013

Responses to Drought

Long shadows cast by the orange sun
Cross the keyboard as my fingers type.
Stone chips on the desert lose the chill of night.
Outside, fruit ripens early, small because of drought.

The other day my friend and I worked hard
Felling trees for winter wood.
He dragged them with his tractor through dry dirt
To the barn to cut them into rounds.
I walked behind him after dust cleared,
Made a few cuts and wet wood chips down.
Smoke from nearby fires drifted in.
I searched for a metaphor to describe what presses.
Grass browned weeks ago.
Bees drink from the birdbath.
That all things live by water becomes clear.
I fill the birdbath early. I water trees.

2021

Breakfast Early

We pick blueberries and plums,
Wash, slice, pour cream, sprinkle sugar,
And with spoons eat slowly.

The outside air is warm
And we wonder about shadows and bird calls
Before we start routines.

If we are wise, we linger.
Not yet, you whisper.
I am listening.

2018

Fall

September

Tree shadows rise dark
Against orange evening sky.
Does either hold meaning?

October

They are leaving,
The birds that painted summer,
Finches and pine siskins flying.

November

November's habits—
Chains on tractor tires,
Crow calls, cold rain.

Overlook

This poem is about thick western clouds,
Rain sweeps not felt for weeks,
The tenacity of trees I watered all summer.

This poem holds the crude basin I made
As a marker for my wife's remains
Spread on a northern hillside
With a meadow view.

The business of going on
Ignores the past a while.
But cast seeds sometimes sprout
And return irregular as rain.

Beyond the window stands an elderberry
Where quail crowd and run.

Some weeks ago, an orange cat showed up,
A cast-off I assumed.
It stays a stranger, spooks when we go out,
Though it stops to look before it flees.

How does the world evolve?
Are quail wary of the stalking cat?

This splurge of thinking passes as I watch—
Concerns about what matters
Enrich the medium of love,
Add texture to the web within.

2021

Boundaries

It is a half year since I called my neighbor
To ask where to send a letter.
I wanted to explain my thoughts on the slough
That spans our boundary and hosts waterfowl every spring.

He flew into a rage,
Telling me he would do what he wanted with his land.
I told him that was not my intent and tried to calm him.
His ire rose no matter what I said.

He told me to talk to him
From my side of the fence,
To which I said again I just wanted to explain
My feelings about the slough.

In mid-sentence he hung up.
I held the phone, the useless thing,
Rattled by his anger.

I still shake as I walk the boundary line,
Dry and clogged with grass this fall.
What will the slough look like
When snow melts next spring?

2021

Yard Inventory

The other day I cleaned birdhouses.
Most were empty, frosted, damp.
Some had wasp nests
Glued to roofs by paper stems.
A few bulged with wren twigs.
Swallow feathers lined two.
One house, the one dad built,
Has a resin coated hole.
Most times nuthatches make their nests
In rotting trunks. For some reason
A pair lives in this small house
Some summers and discreetly carries on.
I clean it every fall to make a home.
Good neighbors get along.

2013

This Evening

Light weakens and firs close in.
Rain beats on metal roof.

Small things compose evening—
Fingers type words one by one.
Small moths bump lit glass.

We move in the kitchen fixing food.
I bake bread and make meatloaf.
You make plum crumble for us both.

Suddenly the lights go out.
A power failure. I hear you move
Calmly through the room.

Before lights blink and we resume.

2021

Crossbedding

I loft the sheet and feel it settle like feathers
On naked skin. I listen to traffic grinding
On the freeway and hear insanity at 5 a.m.
It is too early for madness to begin.
But this is my impression as gears whine and shift.
Day is more momentum than still time.
Yet, outside, swallows call and wings shadow
The curtain. A wren defends
A t-post with its song.

Sunlight winks through curtain folds.
I watch it move. Grinding muffles nearby worlds—
The birds, my own,
Such perishable things.

How Quickly

The doe stumbled to the rhododendron bush
When I disturbed it last night and fell.
I heard weight break branches.
And walked out to ask how she was.

Her eyes looked wondering at mine.
She licked her lips and reclined,
Ears softened, to dry ground.

I left her, hoping she would birth a fawn
And be gone by morning.

Bats traced dark geometry.

In the morning her hooves were splayed and still.
I went out to the bush, spoke
And tapped her hardened neck
Because I feared death and its finality.

2007

Tallies

I finally understand why fall is sadder than spring.
Earth tones subdue greens.
Snow follows rain
And spring's growth is forgotten.

The other day I stood on the porch
And watched yellow leaves fall
Through branches. They dropped one by one
In slow subtraction.

This loss so gradual, so imperceptible
To the vacant eye and mind that do not realize
That life builds by addition not perceived

Until some movement—
When worn leaves drop through dark branches.

2007

Old World Opening

Rain beat the roof last night.
Wind promised it all afternoon.
A cool breeze ended summer.

In the morning dry grass had softened.
The steps held water.

I closed a window to stay warm.
The drought's long spell was broken.

2006

Tree

I stand still under a large tree on clear nights in October
After leaves have fallen, counting stars through limbs.
I do this not from habit but from the need
To find the mystery of being.
I am only a man
Walking between earth and sky a while.
My body fed by hunger yearns, a form of appetite
For what I cannot hold, cannot substantiate,
Which is as real as an apple.
So, I stand below spread branches
And scan with so much wonder
Star patterns overhead.

2015

Meanderings

Walking through the woods
Looking for my splitting maul
That fell off the pickup bed,
I imagined the hickory handle cracked
Because I drove over it
With a heavy load of logs.

That day it was raining
And worn wipers streaked glass
As I wiped fog with a dirty rag
And navigated leaning trunks.

But the maul lay on soaked duff
Beside the cedar grove.

I picked it up.
Cares dropped.
I tested the handle
To see if it would break.

Walking home, I looked at raindrops
Dazzle moss, remembered Faulkner's bear
And the boy hunting it, not seeing it
Until he dropped the gun.

I softly held the maul,
A tool that reduces trees to chunks,
And searched for what amazes—
Wood tangle doused by rain,
Crossed limbs, a wrenched root,
Leaves desultory, drooping.

2011

Variation on the Theme of Soup

I saute sliced onions
And add chopped celery.
Hot butter softens them.
I stir the mix, add broth,
Chunked squash and potatoes,
Some paprika.

I boil and simmer it until the chunks are mush
And blend them smooth,
Then pour it in a pot, stir in cream,
Pepper, salt, and heat the soup slowly.
While I wait, I chop chives
And sip soup from a spoon.
When it's done, I pour
It in a bowl, sprinkle chives,
Tear bread into pieces, spread butter
And dunk.

On a damp fall day
Warm soup provides the sun.

2007

Orchard Girl

Your way is slow, selective.
You pick only what is ripe,
Let growing reach its sweetness.
We watch plums color
As they swell and bend thin limbs.
I prop them up and think about the yield.

While you, content, caress them
Between your thumb and fingers.
It is as if you listen for approval
From each plum before you pick it.

I have learned to savor
And sometimes feel this swell
That tells me plums are not just a crop to box
And weigh with satisfaction
At each season's end.

I listen tenderly.
Each plum holds a story.
Slowed, selectively I pick
Beside you.

Midafternoon, Evening, November

This is the recitation of the feel of things,
Your love ephemeral,
My body less certain of its journey,
Time's goblet spilling more than filling.
In this transit we acquaint, move away.
Memory distorts. Let it not replace
The feel of feathering fingers touching,
Like soliloquies in sighs, the way your weight settles
Tired on the bed, rolls me toward you and we breathe side by side,
Alone as we all are, together beneath covers
In the dark.

2020

Love and a 2N Tractor

Love has little to do with words.
To say "I love you"
Is like a rooster crowing.

I labor on a tractor older than I am,
With its radiator leaking. It used to be,
Before I changed the 6-volt battery to 12,
I would try to start it with a prayer.
One shot, then the slowing grind to silence at 5 a.m.
Even with a 12-volt good fortune is at risk.

So, each fall I labor to make do
And the 2N gives what it has left.
I pull the choke and push the starter button down.
Sparkplugs ignite sprayed gas
And the engine fires or not.

If it runs, it finds rhythm as I play the throttle
To build speed.

Love offers chances in a give-and-take.

2022

To the Woods

I kick the pedal to feed gas
And pull the choke until the engine fires.
The Chevy pickup rolls when I ease out the clutch.
Worn wipers sweep off dew.

I'm headed to the woods across the meadow,
Past the rough-sawn barn where cattle were shot
And bled.

I drive the road where years ago
Cattle trudged past a truck
That hauled hay to the barn.

Life then seemed complete
As days repeated with the sun.

To my left, bees swarm through sunlight over hives.
Beekeepers bring us honey every fall.

The pickup rolls downhill
Through a gap where trees end at the field.

The men who cut and baled hay are dead.
The meadow returns to weeds and trees.
I drive the ruts tires made
And accelerate to climb to woods.

I steer with care through trees.
This is a narrow road where each spring
I clear windfalls to get through.
Routines bind as tight as twine does bales.

2021

Ice Storm

Rain spits ice.
Trees' familiar shapes loom gothic.
The path I know by heart becomes a maze of pauses.
All this as I am walking home in an ice storm.

Above, limbs snap.
They crash through ice crust.
If hearing can be trusted, I zig left,
Then try to find my way back to the path.

The quarter mile from my car to home
Is like an icy sea between a ship and shore.
Each wave subtracts my confidence.
Each tree snap saps recall.

At last, I see a light through branches
And break through ice to reach the porch.

A man may lose his bearings getting home.

2006

On Watching Geese

In November we stood in the meadow.
Wind gusted willy-nilly.
Honking above. You pointed at geese flapping
In vee-formation heading south. All predictable.
Suddenly they circled, rose, resumed,
Climbed higher, rose again,
And reformed the formation.

We stood silent, each thinking we had seen
A miracle, but geese attuned to flight
Knew by instinct they must climb
To continue, so they caught a thermal,
Rode what it delivered higher,
Found another and rose higher,
Until some knowledge told them to go on.

2020

Winter

December

Suddenly a white world,
No animals, many tracks,
Lives passing, drifts.

January

Ground being gone,
Snow swirls around trunks
Like clouds thinning.

February

These strange warm days.
Has winter forgotten cold?
Thorn buds swell.

First Snow

December.
The first snow was predicted.
It rained all afternoon. The wind,
Bowling in the trees,
Slashed drops across glass.

The cat curled deeply in the couch.
Drops turned to ice.
Woodstove metal crackled as it warmed.
I stirred embers and added logs
To make fire glow before I banked it.

The night ahead held sleep
And dreams of past winters.
Each had a night when snow arrived.

At dawn the ground was filigreed
With frozen rain and snow.
Firs were ice shagged.
The cat shivered, yawned.
Last night's ice siege had headed east.
I donned wool clothes and winter boots
And wandered through December.

2007

Languor

This morning perhaps you are idling,
Soft as warm oatmeal.
The cat on your lap yawns, stretches,
Drifts.
The dog's tail whacks your leg.
Its claws clack on hardwood.
It insists on going out,
Passes the cat that swats it leaving.
You stir hot porridge.
Life may be indulged.
Diffused light sifts through glass.
You lull. You are alone.
The dog romps in the yard.
The cat curls down in comfort
Where you sat.

2016

Winter Morning

Crumpling newspaper.
Placing kindling.
A whisked match's hiss.
The fluting flames on paper edges.
The stove door cushions into gasket.
Sparks snap.
Descending footsteps on the stairs.
The refrigerator's click and hum.
Heat pops expanding metal.
A faucet's water rush.
The muffled flow of flames.

2022

Meadow, 6:43 A.M.

I skied out this morning,
Breaking trail to the meadow,
The wafer moon dissolving in dawn's blue—
Last curtain call before the sun showed,
The time between the past and new.
I leaned on poles and looked
At icy crystals on a tan grass blade,
At the footprints of a running mouse.
Wind sifted snow. In the distance a deer watched,
Its front leg lifted, still.

2016

Projections

Snow sifting in the meadow,
The sun out, squinting.

Blue shadows undulate
Through white depressions.
My ears hear a red-tailed hawk.
I look up.

The silhouette glides wide winged
In azure, tilts, finds wind, lofts, veers
From clarity to where forked limbs obscure.

It is easy to conclude, ruin a poem with meaning,
Insist, lose faith in what eyes observe,
Spin syllables to space, be done.

The silent hawk lofts from its limb,
Rises billow-winged and crosses tinted sky,
Disappears, leaves only sensed impressions.

2023

Two Astronomers Ski the Meadow

In the meadow, we speculate
About nebular haze
That coalesces into stars.

Around us fog scarves
Aspen branches frocked with snow
And between our eyes and them
Flakes fall.

The choice is not the ethereal or earth.
For we are here, dressed warmly
For this world. Snow crystals break
On my glove. Silence sounds enormous.
We have crossed the meadow many times before
And know its whispers and its volume.

2017

Full Circle

It is better to give than to . . .
That's not what birds say
As they storm the feeder,
Nuzzle through black hulls, crack husks
And chew seeds.
It looks self-centered,
But I notice cast seeds fall
And a squirrel hops to the windfall
And stuffs its cheeks.
Later, turkeys eye and peck what's scattered.

I check after.
Yes, frayed hulls litter ground,
And though the birds do not intend to give,
Acts complete a circle nonetheless.

2015

On This Morning

I glimmer what the old man meant
When he wondered if next year on this date
He would watch again snow falling amid trees,
See deer prints darken snow,
Hear a chickadee's slow calls.

2015

All This

The yard light comes on
As two deer, hungry on a winter night,
Move snow aside for grass.

I thought to toss out apples.
But wild things are not like us who fret.

They wandered in.
They'll wander off.

My Mother-in-Law

The tractor stalled in knee-deep snow.
It was 1 a.m. and the blizzard swirled.
I turned off the lights
And walked toward the farmhouse
Where Marguerite's lights blazed.

She was an insomniac who stayed up nights
Playing honky-tonk piano
Between cookie batches.

I knocked. The music stopped,
And she stared out the window.
I waved and yelled that the tractor stalled
At the bottom of the drive.

She let me in, and I warmed my rear
At the woodstove.

I asked her to hold a flashlight
While I removed the carburetor bowl.

At 2 a.m. we drove to the Chevron station
To blow grunt from a jet.
I held the carburetor
And blew air into it and on my fingers.
Ice never felt so cold.

We drove back to the tractor
And reassembled it.
With a six-volt battery you had few chances
To start the engine.

Marguerite stood aside
As I pulled the choke and pressed the starter button.
The engine fired, died,
Fired again and slowly ran
As I drove the limping tractor home.

2009

Onward

Last Morning

On my last morning
I want to wake early and watch
Sunlight spray through fog and pines.
I want to flow in swallow glides,
Make pinpoints in air and dive
To savor flying's feeling.
I will not rummage memory,
Though it will draw,
But be present as light closes.

2020

Light Left the Meadow

All afternoon light left the meadow.

The farmer noticed this while looking at poplars
Standing like green fans at the fence line
And the way puffed clouds lost edges into blue.

His work on the baler pulled him from observations
To adjust twine tension.

The dog ran beside the hay rows he cut
And pounced at movements.

He noticed light going when he searched in the baler
For a spring his fingers found
And felt the urge to lie down
And listen to the rhythms that the baler disallowed.

Overhead, a red-tailed hawk fanned its feathers against the light.
The dog began whimpering for home.

The farmer looked across the field where dew was settling
And put his tools in his truck.
The windrows should be turned soon, he thought,
As he turned on his lights and drove through darkness
Into dips and out where the dog ran.

Days End

Days end like this with sun washing trees green-gold,
With a mourning dove's near but secret call,
With grass that grows all day bowing gradually to dew
And a purple thistle flower growing slowly into bloom.

The dog ambles over ground after her nose.
She stops and peers into an empty hole.
I hear pots clanging in the kitchen.
No wind sways leaves.

On days like this the world is timeless.
Patterns run a cycle and resume.
The mourning dove lands on the birdbath
And like a maiden bathes and leaves unseen.

I talk to you about the day.
You say it was a costly one.
The cat's fixed broken leg, you mean.
Two weeks from now she'll scramble up the same limb she fell from.

Days end like this with daylight dampening to dark,
With the outside held in check by household light,
And the thought that soon and again tomorrow
The dog will paw the screen to come inside.

1994

On This Day

I light a candle and place it in the window
Even though it is day
To tell the world but most of all myself
About renewal.

2013

Acknowledgment

I appreciate the encouragement, advice and editing of Theresa Shaffer, Barry Grimes, Jim Bodeen and Chris DeForest, and the support and hard work of publisher Doug Johnson. Without their help, these poems would have remained rough drafts.

About the Author

Wes Hanson grew up in Michigan and worked as a carpenter to pay for college. He taught high school English there for three years before pedaling a bicycle across Canada and attending graduate school at the University of Idaho where he met his wife. They designed and built their home on the farm described in the poems.

Together, they worked on the Hanford nuclear site cleanup as part of a citizens' advisory group and were involved in county land use planning. He continued this work after she died, helping the county write comprehensive plans and serving as the county planning commission chairman.

They also spearheaded a successful effort to keep the land around Lake Coeur d'Alene's Cougar Bay from being developed. This was ultimately accomplished through land purchases by The Idaho Nature Conservancy and the Bureau of Land Management and a conservation easement negotiated by the Inland Northwest Land Conservancy. An account of this campaign is found in Theresa Shaffer's book, *Cougar Bay Nature Preserve: Saving Coeur d'Alene's Natural Gem*, published by The History Press in 2023. Hanson edited this book. For readers interested in supporting efforts to preserve natural areas, tax-deductible contributions can be sent to the Inland Northwest Land Conservancy (INLC) at 35 W. Main Ave., Suite 210, Spokane, WA 99201 or to a land trust in their area. INLC is a 501 (c) (3) organization.

Hanson taught college prep literature at a north Idaho high school for thirty years. During that time, he took part in various National Endowment for the Humanities (NEH) seminars and represented Idaho as its NEH Teacher-Scholar. Many of the studies concerned America's turbulent racial and civil rights history. In addition, he edited seven student-written publications on the writing process and reading and writing about literature.

Hanson has published a few poems and writes regularly. He also paints and teaches drawing and painting. The Illustrations in this book are his, arranged by their locations in the book, titles, dates and mediums as follows:

Front Cover: "Old Companions" 2015 (Watercolor)
Spring: "Chickadee" 2019 (Pencil)
Summer: "Meadow Home" 2010 (Watercolor)
Fall: "Remains" 2020 (Pencil)
Winter: "Winter Gate" 2023 (Ink)
Back Cover: "Anchors" 2024 (Watercolor)

Currently, Wes and his partner Theresa are learning to identify birds that visit the farm.

www.ingramcontent.com/pod-product-compliance
Lightning Source LLC
Chambersburg PA
CBHW041308020426
42333CB00006B/67